rockschool®

Bass
Technical Handbook

Every Technical Exercise you need for Rockschool examinations printed in full

Acknowledgements

Published by Rockschool Ltd. © 2012
Catalogue Number RSK111205
ISBN: 978-1-908920-32-4

AUDIO
Recorded, mixed and mastered at Langlei Studios by Duncan Jordan
Producer: James Uings

MUSICIANS
Stuart Clayton, Fergus Gerrand, Noam Lederman, Kit Morgan, Stuart Ryan, Ross Stanley

PUBLISHING
Music engraving and book layout by Simon Troup and Jennie Troup of Digital Music Art
Proof and copy editing by Stephen Lawson, Simon Pitt, James Uings and Stuart Clayton
Cover design by Philip Millard
Cover photography by Adam Gasson

SYLLABUS
Syllabus director: Jeremy Ward
Instrumental specialists: Stuart Clayton, Noam Lederman and James Uings

SPONSORSHIP
Noam Lederman plays Mapex Drums, PAISTE cymbals and uses Vic Firth Sticks
Rockschool would like to thank the following companies for donating instruments used in the cover artwork

PRINTING
Printed and bound in the United Kingdom by Caligraving Ltd
CDs manufactured in the European Union by Software Logistics

DISTRIBUTION
Exclusive Distributors: Music Sales Ltd

CONTACTING ROCKSCHOOL
www.rockschool.co.uk
Telephone: +44 (0)845 460 4747
Fax: +44 (0)845 460 1960

Table of Contents

Introductions & Information

Page

Technical Exercises

Welcome to the Rockschool Bass *Technical Handbook*

In this book you will find printed in full all the scales and arpeggios needed to complete the Technical Exercises section of Rockschool's Bass grade exams.

This book should be read in conjunction with the relevant grade books (Debut–Grade 8) published by Rockschool and the *Syllabus Guide* for Bass. The *Syllabus Guide* can be downloaded for free from our website: *www.rockschool.co.uk*.

In the Rockschool grade exam system, the Technical Exercises form the core of each grade. Mastering them gives players a valuable insight not only into the types of scales and arpeggios needed for any improvisational work they may be required to do, but also into the other types of 'unseen' tests they will encounter in the exam, such as the Sight Reading, Improvisation & Interpretation and Ear Tests, and at Grade 6 or higher, the Quick Study Piece.

This book is divided and ordered by grade, starting with Debut and then progressing from Grade 1 to Grade 8. Its many features include the following:

- At the start of the book we have included some Frequently Asked Questions which we hope will cover the enquiry topics most commonly sent in to the Rockschool office by teachers and learners.

- A grade-by-grade ordering of technical material showing all the keys, starting notes and fingering patterns for the scales and arpeggios needed to complete the exam.

- Each section is introduced by a page which summarises the content found in each grade. These pages show what's new grade-by-grade as well as showing, at a glance, the technical work required for each grade.

- At Grades 6–8 the Technical Exercises conclude with a Stylistic Study. Candidates may choose one of the three Studies to perform in the exam. Please note that the choice of style in the Study will dictate the style of the Quick Study Piece.

We hope you find this book useful and that it will inspire you to approach the Technical Exercises in our exams without fear. To make best use of it, you will need a bass in standard tuning and either a physical or a virtual metronome which can be downloaded as a phone app for very little cost.

Frequently Asked Questions

What are the examiners looking for?

The examiners are looking for fluency, accuracy and promptness of response. The assessment requirements for the Technical Exercises for each grade can be found in the *Syllabus Guide* for Bass, available at *www.rockschool.co.uk*.

Will I have to play all the exercises listed in the exam?

At most grades, no. The examiner will usually ask you to perform a selection of the listed exercises at each grade. However, at Debut and Grade 1 there are fewer questions and, therefore, the examiner may ask you to play all of them.

Will I be asked to perform any exercise from a grade lower than the one I am attempting?

No. You will be only be asked to play the exercises printed in the grade book.

What does ♩=80 mean?

This is the tempo (speed) that the exercise is to be played at. If the exercise does not have a backing track you can use a metronome to indicate the tempo at which the exercise is to be played. A metronome is a device that provides a steady pulse to help you ensure that you play at a consistent tempo. Teachers often recommend that students buy a metronome as they are also useful in helping to build speed towards the final required tempo.

Do I have to use a metronome in the exam?

No. However, before you start the section you will be asked if you would like to play the exercises along with the click or hear a single bar of click before you commence the test.

What should I do if I make a mistake?

Stay calm and do your best to recover and carry on. The examiner is there to award marks for what you can do, not penalise you for what you can't.

Can I take this book into the exam?

No. The only book a candidate is allowed to take into a Rockschool examination is the grade book appropriate for the examination being taken.

Can I have my grade book open at the relevant page of Technical Exercises in the exam?

Yes.

Bass Notation Explained

THE MUSICAL STAVE shows pitches and rhythms and is divided by lines into bars. Pitches are named after the first seven letters of the alphabet.

TABLATURE graphically represents the bass guitar fingerboard. Each horizontal line represents a string and each number represents a fret.

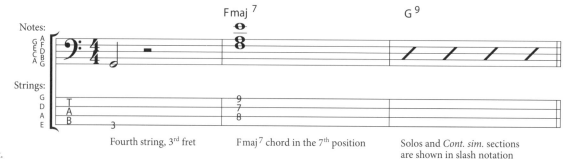

Fourth string, 3rd fret   Fmaj7 chord in the 7th position   Solos and *Cont. sim.* sections are shown in slash notation

Definitions For Special Bass Guitar Notation

HAMMER-ON: Pick the lower note then sound the higher note by fretting it without picking.

PULL-OFF: Pick the higher note then sound the lower note by lifting your finger without picking.

SLIDE: Pick the first note and slide to the next. If the line connects (as below) the second note is *not* repicked.

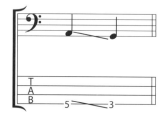

GLISSANDO: Slide off of a note at the end of its rhythmic value. The note that follows *is* repicked.

SLAP STYLE: Slap bass technique is indicated through the letters T (thumb) and P (pull).

TAPPING: Sound note by tapping the string – circles denote a picking hand tap, squares a fretting hand tap.

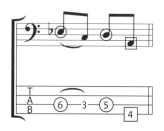

DEAD (GHOST) NOTES: Pick the string while the note is muted by your fretting hand.

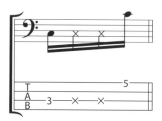

NATURAL HARMONICS: Lightly touch the string above the indicated fret then pick to sound a harmonic.

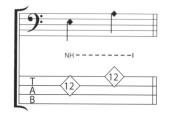

 (accent)   ▪ Accentuate note (play it louder).

 (staccato)   ▪ Shorten time value of note.

    ▪ Fermata (Pause)

D.%. al Coda   ▪ Go back to the sign (%), then play until the bar marked To Coda ⊕ then skip to the section marked ⊕ Coda.

D.C. al Fine   ▪ Go back to the beginning of the song and play until the bar marked Fine (end).

   ▪ Repeat bars between signs.

   ▪ When a repeated section has different endings, play the first ending only the first time and the second ending only the second time.

Debut

Debut features two scales and arpeggios in two keys. They are both in open position, which is the open strings and first four frets of the bass. At the end of the Technical Exercises you will play a riff to a backing track. The first bar of the riff is notated in full and you will have to move the pattern to the correct starting note in the remaining, un-notated bars.

Technical Work	
Tempo	♩ = 70
Scales | Major	E & A
Scales | Minor Pentatonic	E & A
Arpeggios | Major	E & A
Arpeggios | Minor	E & A
Riff	Four bars @ ♩ = 70

Debut Technical Exercises

Group A: Scales | Major scales

1. E major

2. A major

Group A: Scales | Minor pentatonic scales

1. E minor pentatonic

2. A minor pentatonic

Group B: Arpeggios | Major arpeggios

1. E major

2. A major

Group B: Arpeggios | Minor arpeggios

1. E minor

2. A minor

Group C | Riff

In the exam you will be asked to play the following riff to a backing track. The riff shown in bar 1 should be played in the same shape in bars 2–4. The root note of the pattern to be played is shown in the music in each of the subsequent three bars.

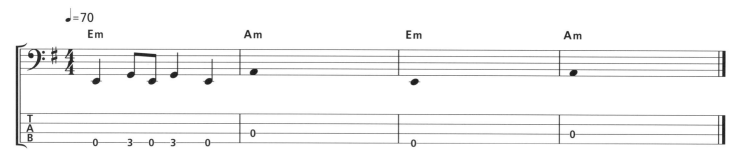

Grade 1

Grade 1 adds two new scale types and a third key to those covered at Debut. The new scale types are the natural minor and major pentatonic scales. The arpeggio types remain the same (major and minor) but include a higher octave of the root note and a third key. The riff exercise follows the same procedure as the Debut exam.

Technical Work

Tempo	♩ = 70
Scales | Major	E, A & G
Scales | Minor Pentatonic	E, A & G
Scales | Natural Minor	E, A & G
Scales | Major Pentatonic	E, A & G
Arpeggios | Major	E, A & G
Arpeggios | Minor	E, A & G
Riff	Four bars @ ♩ = 70

Grade 1 Technical Exercises

Group A: Scales | Major scales

1. E major

2. A major

3. G major

Group A: Scales | Minor pentatonic scales

1. E minor pentatonic

2. A minor pentatonic

3. G minor pentatonic

Grade 1 Technical Exercises

Group A: Scales | Natural minor scales

1. E natural minor

2. A natural minor

3. G natural minor

Group A: Scales | Major pentatonic scales

1. E major pentatonic

2. A major pentatonic

3. G major pentatonic

Grade 1 Technical Exercises

Group B: Arpeggios | Major arpeggios

1. E major

2. A major

3. G major

Group B: Arpeggios | Minor arpeggios

1. E minor

2. A minor

3. G minor

Group C | Riff

CD Track 2

In the exam you will be asked to play the following riff to a backing track. The riff shown in bar 1 should be played in the same shape in bars 2–4. The root note of the pattern to be played is shown in the music in each of the subsequent three bars.

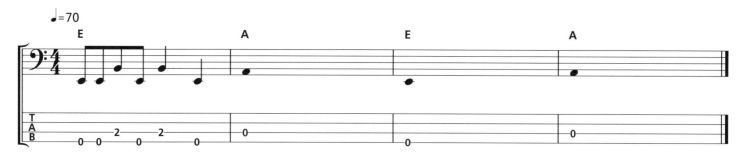

Grade 2

Grade 2 uses the same four scale types as Grade 1. The arpeggio types are also unchanged. Although there are still three keys at Grade 2, these are slightly different from Grade 1. The riff exercise is now based on a two-bar pattern and the test lasts for eight bars rather than four.

Technical Work	
Tempo	♩ = 80
Scales | Major	A, G & C
Scales | Natural Minor	A, G & C
Scales | Minor Pentatonic	A, G & C
Scales | Major Pentatonic	A, G & C
Arpeggios | Major	A, G & C
Arpeggios | Minor	A, G & C
Riff	Eight bars @ ♩ = 80

Grade 2 Technical Exercises

Group A: Scales | Major scales

1. A major

2. G major

3. C major

Group A: Scales | Natural minor scales

1. A natural minor

2. G natural minor

3. C natural minor

Grade 2 Technical Exercises

Group A: Scales | Minor pentatonic scales

1. A minor pentatonic

2. G minor pentatonic

3. C minor pentatonic

Group A: Scales | Major pentatonic scales

1. A major pentatonic

2. G major pentatonic

3. C major pentatonic

Grade 2 Technical Exercises

Group B: Arpeggios | Major arpeggios

1. A major

2. G major

3. C major

Group B: Arpeggios | Minor arpeggios

1. A minor

2. G minor

3. C minor

Group C | Riff

In the exam you will be asked to play the following riff to a backing track. The riff shown in bars 1 and 2 should be played in the same shape in bars 3–8. The root note of the pattern to be played is shown in the music in bars 3, 5 and 7.

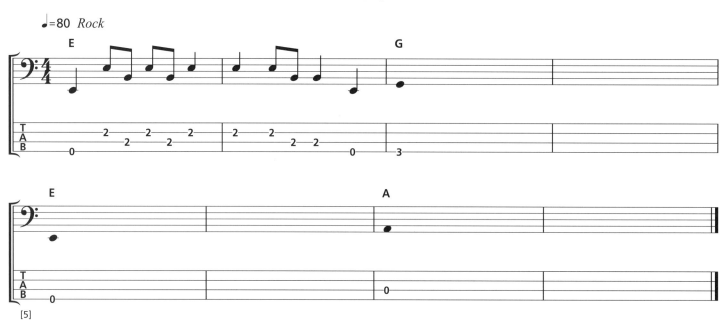

Grade 3

Grade 3 adds the blues scale to the four scale types in Grade 2. A third arpeggio type (dominant[7]) is added to the major and minor arpeggios found in previous grades. The scale and arpeggios are required in three keys. The riff exercise follows the same format as Grade 2, but the tempo is increased to ♩= 90 and uses more eighth notes.

Technical Work	
Tempo	♩=90
Scales | Major	G, A & B
Scales | Natural Minor	G, A & B
Scales | Minor Pentatonic	G, A & B
Scales | Major Pentatonic	G, A & B
Scales | Blues	G, A & B
Arpeggios | Major	G, A & B
Arpeggios | Minor	G, A & B
Arpeggios | Dominant[7]	G, A & B
Riff	Eight bars @ ♩=90

Grade 3 Technical Exercises

Group A: Scales | Major scales

1. G major scale

2. A major scale

3. B major scale

Group A: Scales | Natural minor scales

1. G natural minor scale

2. A natural minor scale

3. B natural minor scale

Grade 3 Technical Exercises

Group A: Scales | Minor pentatonic scales

1. G minor pentatonic scale

2. A minor pentatonic scale

3. B minor pentatonic scale

Group A: Scales | Major pentatonic scales

1. G major pentatonic scale

2. A major pentatonic scale

3. B major pentatonic scale

Grade 3 Technical Exercises

Group A: Scales | Blues scales

1. G blues scale

2. A blues scale

3. B blues scale

Group B: Arpeggios | Major arpeggios

1. G major arpeggio

2. A major arpeggio

3. B major arpeggio

Grade 3 Technical Exercises

Group B: Arpeggios | Minor arpeggios

1. G minor arpeggio

2. A minor arpeggio

3. B minor arpeggio

Group B: Arpeggios | Dominant⁷ arpeggios

1. G dominant⁷ arpeggio

2. A dominant⁷ arpeggio

3. B dominant⁷ arpeggio

Group C | Riff

CD Track 4

In the exam you will be asked to play the following riff to a backing track. The riff shown in bars 1 and 2 should be played in the same shape in bars 3–8. The root note of the pattern to be played is shown in the music in bars 3, 5 and 7.

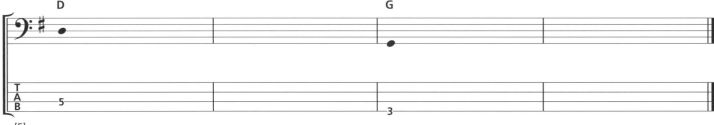

[5]

Grade 4

Grade 4 uses the five scale types from Grade 3; however, the major and minor pentatonic scales are in keys that require the use of open strings. The remaining three scale types and the arpeggios are required in four keys. The tempo of the riff exercise increases to ♩ = 100 and uses eighth-note rests.

Technical Work	
Tempo	♩ = 80 (♫ played)
Scales	Natural Minor	A, B, C & D
Scales	Minor Pentatonic	A, B, C & D
Scales	Blues	A, B, C & D
Scales	Major	F & A♯/B♭
Scales	Major Pentatonic	F & A♯/B♭
Arpeggios	Major	A, B, C & D
Arpeggios	Minor	A, B, C & D
Arpeggios	Dominant [7]	A, B, C & D
Riff	Eight bars @ ♩ = 100

Grade 4 Technical Exercises

Group A: Scales | Natural minor scales

1. A natural minor scale

2. B natural minor scale

3. C natural minor scale

4. D natural minor scale

Group A: Scales | Minor pentatonic scales

1. A minor pentatonic scale

2. B minor pentatonic scale

3. C minor pentatonic scale

4. D minor pentatonic scale

Grade 4 Technical Exercises

Group A: Scales | Blues scales

1. A blues scale

2. B blues scale

3. C blues scale

4. D blues scale

Group A: Scales | Major scales

1. F major scale

2. B♭ major scale

Grade 4 Technical Exercises

Group A: Scales | Major pentatonic scales

1. F major pentatonic scale

2. B♭ major pentatonic scale

Group B: Arpeggios | Major arpeggios

1. A major arpeggio

2. B major arpeggio

3. C major arpeggio

4. D major arpeggio

Grade 4 Technical Exercises

Group B: Arpeggios | Minor arpeggios

1. A minor arpeggio

2. B minor arpeggio

3. C minor arpeggio

4. D minor arpeggio

Group B: Arpeggios | Dominant⁷ arpeggios

1. A dominant⁷ arpeggio

2. B dominant⁷ arpeggio

3. C dominant⁷ arpeggio

4. D dominant⁷ arpeggio

Group C | Riff

CD Track 5

In the exam you will be asked to play the following riff to a backing track. The riff shown in bars 1 and 2 should be played in the same shape in bars 3–8. The root note of the pattern to be played is shown in the music in bars 3, 5 and 7.

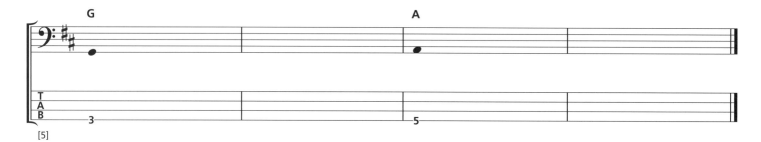

[5]

Grade 5

Grade 5 adds a sixth scale type (harmonic minor) to the five found in previous grades. All scales must be played in two specified fingerboard positions. Two arpeggio types (major ^{7} and minor ^{7}) are added to the three covered in Grades 3 and 4. All scales and arpeggios are required in four keys. The riff exercise introduces 16th notes.

Technical Work

Tempo	♩=80 (♫ played)
Scales | Major	G, A♯/B♭, C & D
Scales | Major Pentatonic	G, A♯/B♭, C & D
Scales | Natural Minor	G, A♯/B♭, C & D
Scales | Minor Pentatonic	G, A♯/B♭, C & D
Scales | Blues	G, A♯/B♭, C & D
Scales | Harmonic Minor	G, A♯/B♭, C & D
Arpeggios | Major	G, A♯/B♭, C & D
Arpeggios | Minor	G, A♯/B♭, C & D
Arpeggios | Dominant ^{7}	G, A♯/B♭, C & D
Arpeggios | Major ^{7}	G, A♯/B♭, C & D
Arpeggios | Minor ^{7}	G, A♯/B♭, C & D
Riff	Eight bars @ ♩=100

Grade 5 Technical Exercises

Group A: Scales | Major scales

1. G major scale

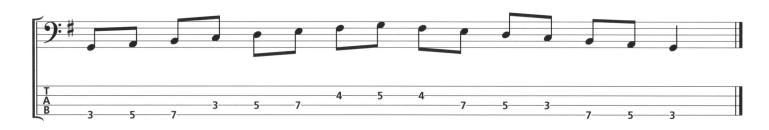

2. B♭ major scale

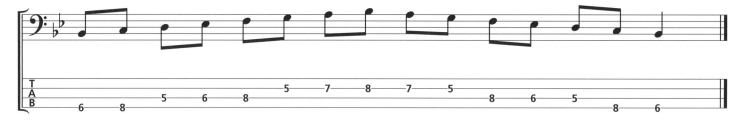

3. C major scale

4. D major scale

Grade 5 Technical Exercises

Group A: Scales | Major pentatonic scales

1. G major pentatonic scale

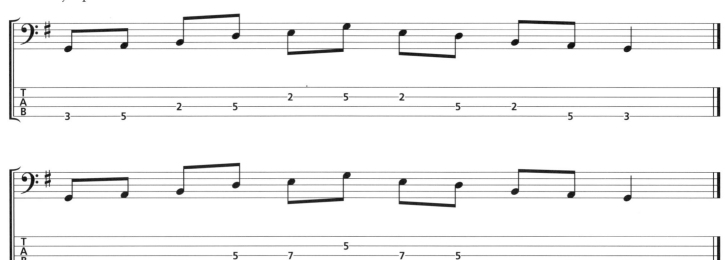

2. B♭ major pentatonic scale

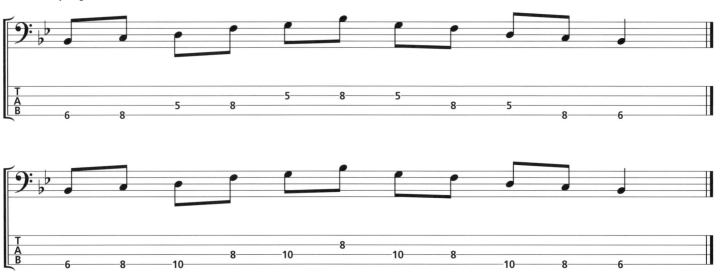

3. C major pentatonic scale

4. D major pentatonic scale

Grade 5 Technical Exercises

Group A: Scales | Natural minor scales

1. G natural minor scale

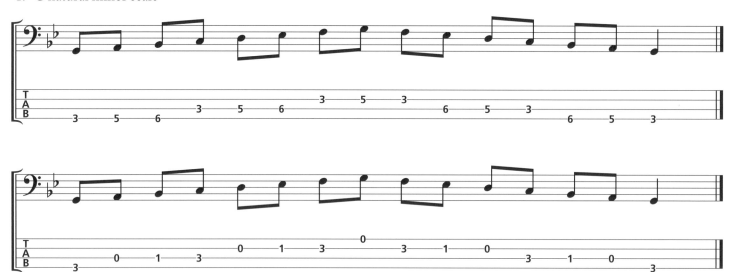

2. B♭ natural minor scale

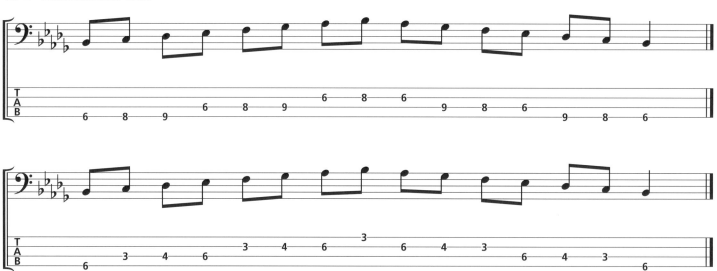

3. C natural minor scale

4. D natural minor scale

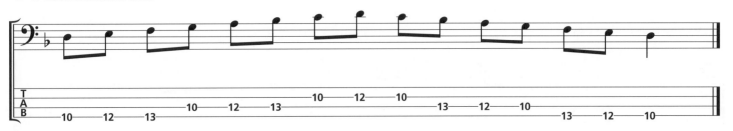

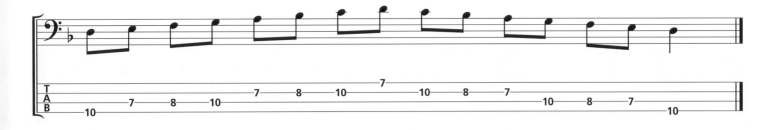

Grade 5 Technical Exercises

Group A: Scales | Minor pentatonic scales

1. G minor pentatonic scale

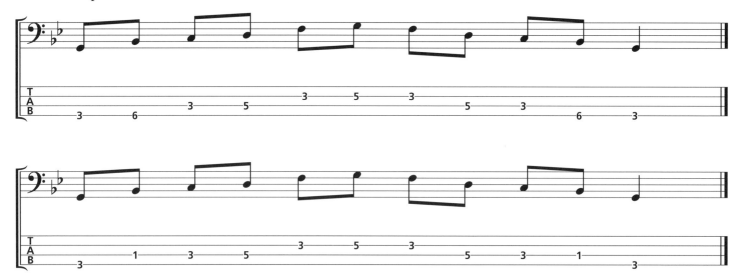

2. B♭ minor pentatonic scale

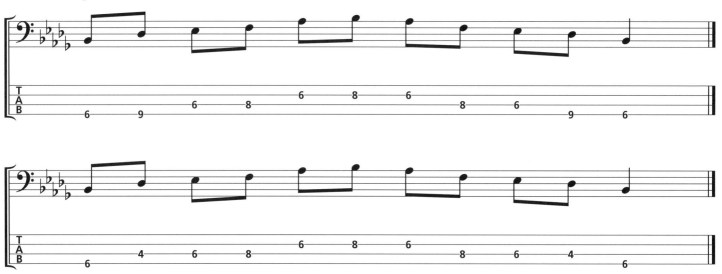

3. C minor pentatonic scale

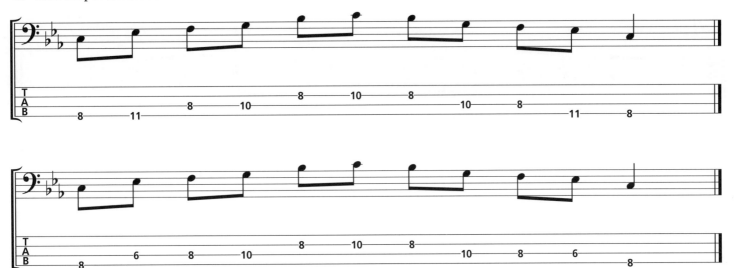

4. D minor pentatonic scale

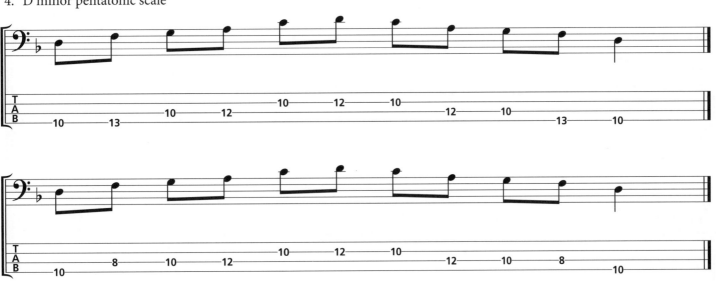

Grade 5 Technical Exercises

Group A: Scales | Blues scales

1. G blues scale

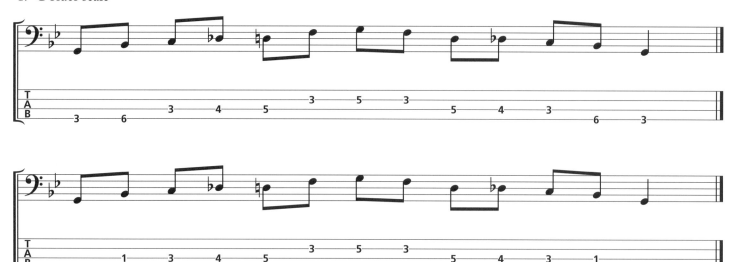

2. B♭ blues scale

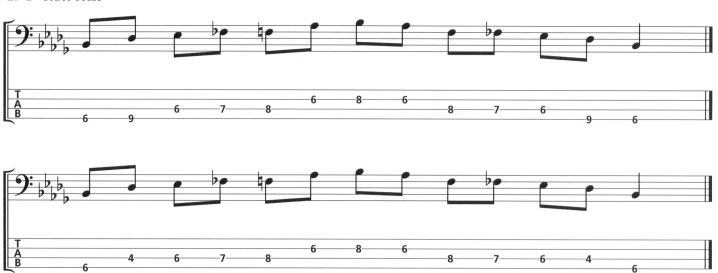

3. C blues scale

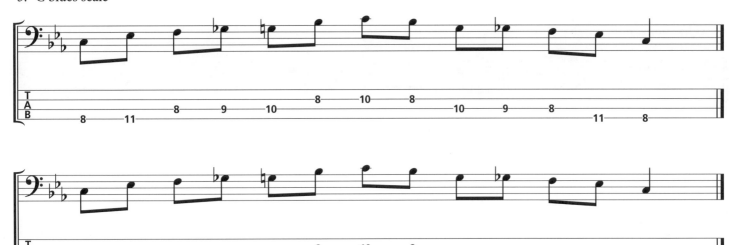

4. D blues scale

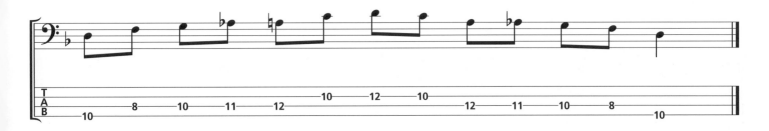

Grade 5 Technical Exercises

Group A: Scales | Harmonic minor scales

1. G harmonic minor scale

2. B♭ harmonic minor scale

3. C harmonic minor scale

4. D harmonic minor scale

Grade 5 Technical Exercises

Group B: Arpeggios | Major arpeggios

1. G major arpeggio

2. B♭ major arpeggio

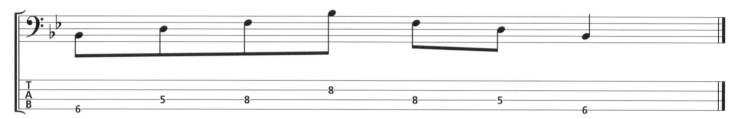

3. C major arpeggio

4. D major arpeggio

Group B: Arpeggios | Minor arpeggios

1. G minor arpeggio

2. B♭ minor arpeggio

3. C minor arpeggio

4. D minor arpeggio

Grade 5 Technical Exercises

Group B: Arpeggios | Dominant⁷ arpeggios

1. G dominant⁷ arpeggio

2. B♭ dominant⁷ arpeggio

3. C dominant⁷ arpeggio

4. D dominant⁷ arpeggio

Group B: Arpeggios | Major⁷ arpeggios

1. G major⁷ arpeggio

2. B♭ major⁷ arpeggio

3. C major⁷ arpeggio

4. D major⁷ arpeggio

Grade 5 Technical Exercises

Group B: Arpeggios | Minor⁷ arpeggios

1. G minor⁷ arpeggio

2. B♭ minor⁷ arpeggio

3. C minor⁷ arpeggio

4. D minor⁷ arpeggio

Group C | Riff

In the exam you will be asked to play the following riff to a backing track. The riff shown in bars 1 and 2 should be played in the same shape in bars 3–8. The root note of the pattern to be played is shown in the music in bars 3, 5 and 7.

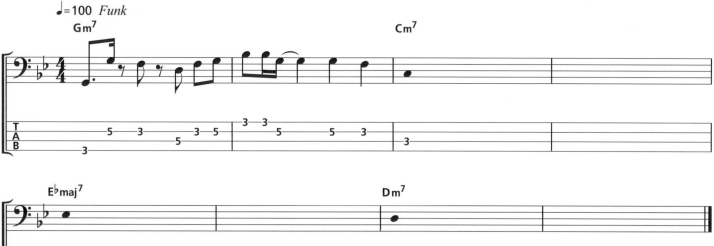

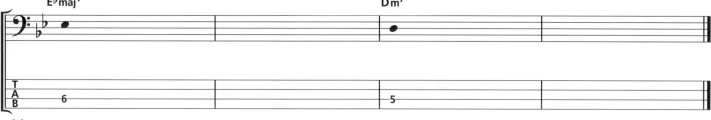

[5]

Grade 6

Grade 6 is very different from Grade 5. It features two modes (dorian and mixolydian) in two fingerings from four starting notes. The minor pentatonic scale is now required in five fingerboard shapes in two keys. Two new arpeggio types (diminished and minor$^{7\flat5}$) are required from four starting notes. Two chord types (dominant^7 and minor^7) are also added. The riff exercise has been replaced by a choice of three Stylistic Studies which are played to a backing track.

Technical Work	
Tempo	$\quarternote = 100$ ($\eighthnote\eighthnote$ played)
Modes | Dorian	E, F, G & A
Modes | Mixolydian	E, F, G & A
Scales | Minor Pentatonic	G & B in five shapes
Arpeggios | Minor $^{7\flat5}$	E, F, G & A
Arpeggios | Diminished	E, F, G & A
Chords | Dominant ^{7}	F & G
Chords | Minor ^{7}	F & G
Stylistic Studies	Rock/Metal Funk Jazz/Latin/Blues

Grade 6 Technical Exercises

Group A: Modes | Dorian mode

1. E dorian mode

2. F dorian mode

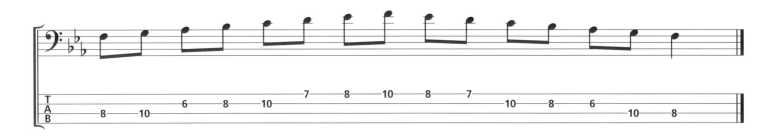

3. G dorian mode

4. A dorian mode

Grade 6 Technical Exercises

Group A: Modes | Mixolydian mode

1. E mixolydian mode

2. F mixolydian mode

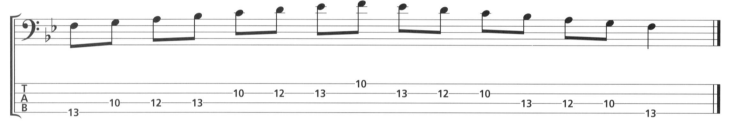

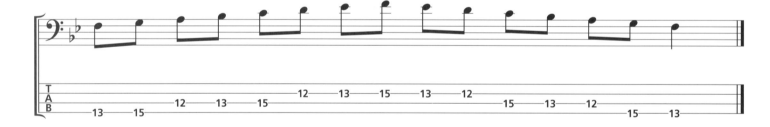

3. G mixolydian mode

4. A mixolydian mode

Group B: Scales | G minor pentatonic scale

1. G minor pentatonic scale, shape 1

2. G minor pentatonic scale, shape 2

3. G minor pentatonic scale, shape 3

4. G minor pentatonic scale, shape 4

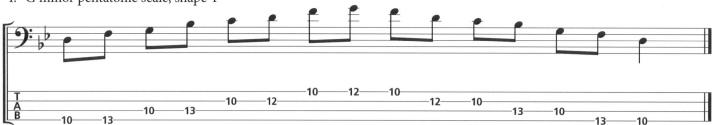

5. G minor pentatonic scale, shape 5

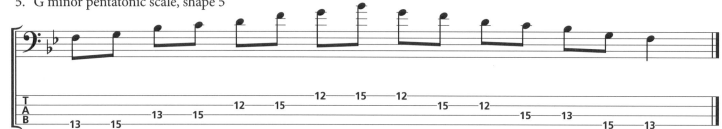

Group B: Scales | B minor pentatonic scale

1. B minor pentatonic scale, shape 1

2. B minor pentatonic scale, shape 2

3. B minor pentatonic scale, shape 3

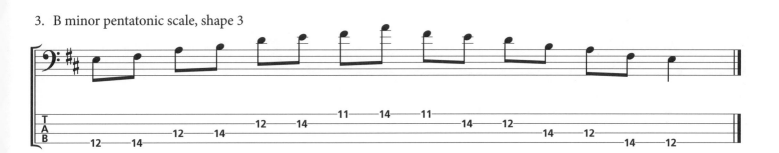

4. B minor pentatonic scale, shape 4

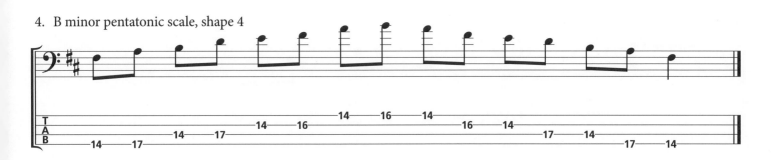

5. B minor pentatonic scale, shape 5

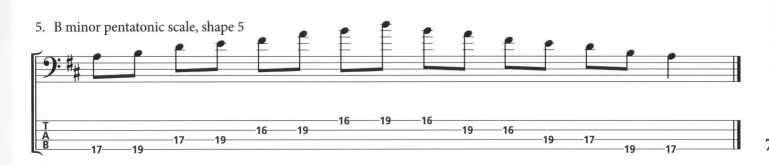

Grade 6 Technical Exercises

Group C: Arpeggios | Minor $7^{\flat}5$ arpeggios

1. E minor $7^{\flat}5$

2. F minor $7^{\flat}5$

3. G minor $7^{\flat}5$

4. A minor $7^{\flat}5$

Group C: Arpeggios | Diminished arpeggios

1. E diminished

2. F diminished

3. G diminished

4. A diminished

Group D: Chords | Dominant⁷ chords

1. F dominant^7

2. G dominant^7

Group D: Chords | Minor⁷ chords

1. F minor⁷

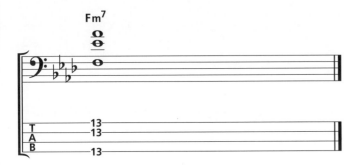

2. G minor⁷

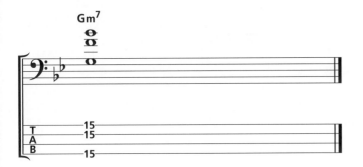

Grade 6 Technical Exercises

Group E: Stylistic Studies

You will prepare a technical study from one group of styles from the list below. Your choice of style will determine the style of the Quick Study Piece.

1. Rock/Metal: 16th-note fingerstyle grooves and legato playing

CD Tracks 7 & 8

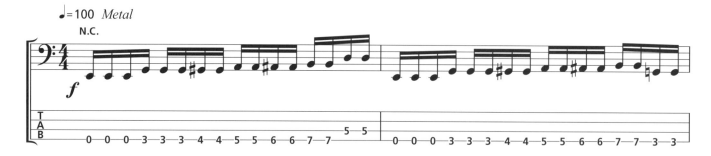

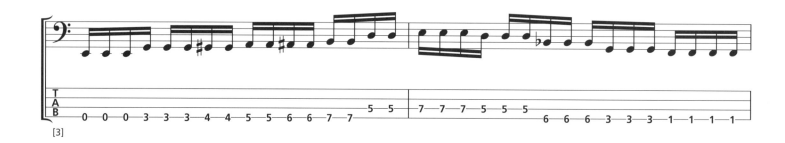

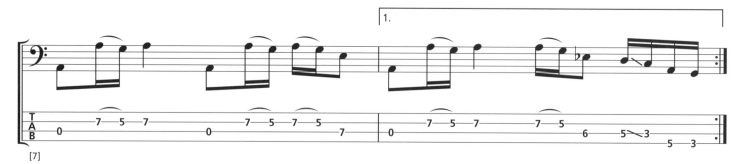

2. Funk: slap and pop playing and percussive 16ᵗʰ-note fingerstyle playing

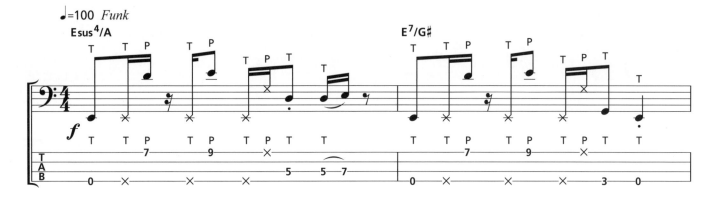

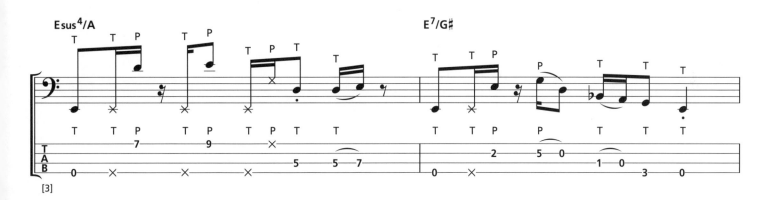

[3]

[5]

[7]

3. Jazz/Latin/Blues: chords and upper register playing

CD Tracks 11 & 12

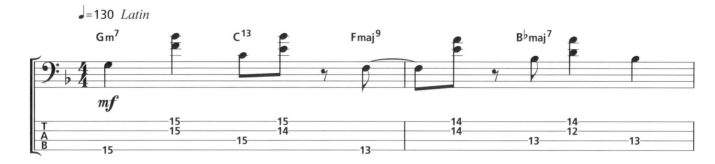

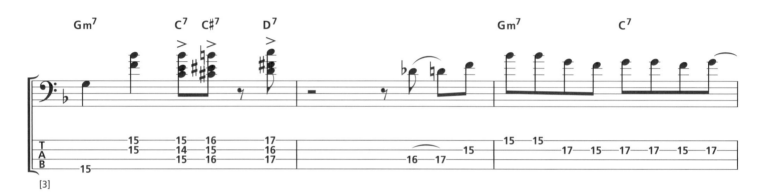

[3]

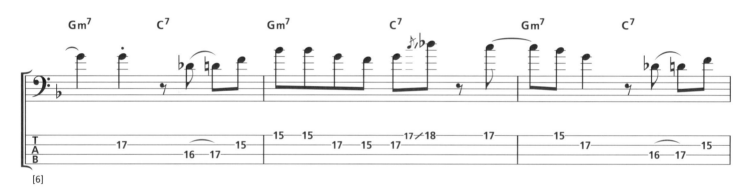

[6]

[9]

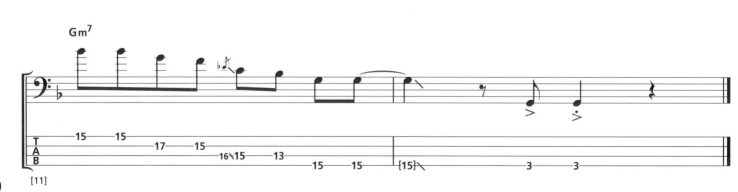

[11]

Grade 7

Grade 7 features two new modes (lydian and phrygian) and the jazz melodic minor scale in two fingerings from four different starting notes. The major scale is required over two octaves in one key. Three new arpeggios (major ^{9}, minor ^{9} and dominant ^{9}) from four starting notes are also required. A third chord type (major ^{7}) is added to the two covered in Grade 6. The Stylistic Studies follow the same procedure as Grade 6.

Technical Work

Tempo	$\quad$ = 100 ($\quad$ played)
Modes | Lydian	F, A#/B♭, D & D#/E♭
Modes | Phrygian	F, A#/B♭, D & D#/E♭
Modes | Jazz Melodic Minor	F, A#/B♭, D & D#/E♭
Scales | Major	G
Arpeggios | Major ^{9}	F, A#/B♭, D & D#/E♭
Arpeggios | Minor ^{9}	F, A#/B♭, D & D#/E♭
Arpeggios | Dominant ^{9}	F, A#/B♭, D & D#/E♭
Chords | Dominant ^{7}	E & A
Chords | Minor ^{7}	E & A
Chords | Major ^{7}	E & A
Stylistic Studies	Rock/Metal Funk Jazz/Latin/Blues

Grade 7 Technical Exercises

Group A: Modes | Lydian mode

1. F lydian mode

2. B♭ lydian mode

3. D lydian mode

4. E♭ lydian mode

Grade 7 Technical Exercises

Group A: Modes | Phrygian mode

1. F phrygian mode

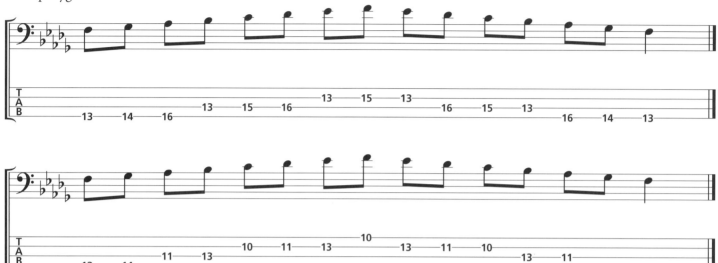

2. B♭ phrygian mode

3. D phrygian mode

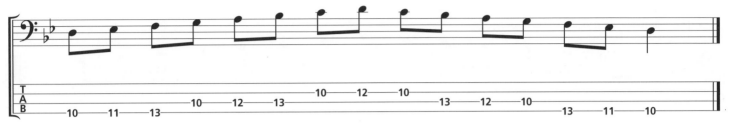

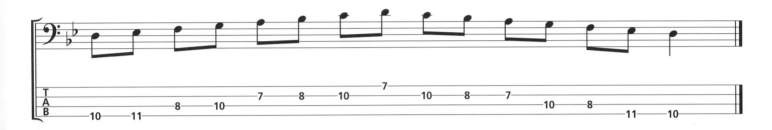

4. E♭ phrygian mode

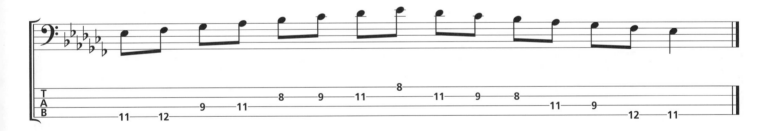

Grade 7 Technical Exercises

Group A: Modes | Jazz melodic minor scale

1. F jazz melodic minor scale

2. B♭ jazz melodic minor scale

3. D jazz melodic minor scale

4. E♭ jazz melodic minor scale

Group B: Scales | Major scales

1. G major scale

Group C: Arpeggios | Major⁹ arpeggios

1. F major⁹ arpeggio

2. B♭ major⁹ arpeggio

3. D major⁹ arpeggio

4. E♭ major⁹ arpeggio

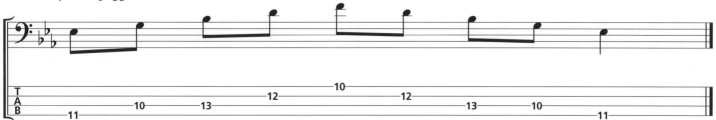

Group C: Arpeggios | Minor⁹ arpeggios

1. F minor⁹ arpeggio

2. B♭ minor⁹ arpeggio

3. D minor⁹ arpeggio

4. E♭ minor⁹ arpeggio

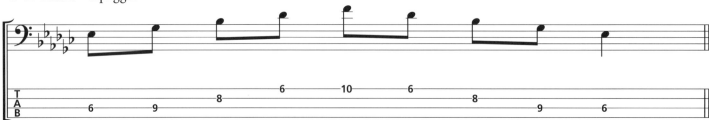

Group C: Arpeggios | Dominant ^{9} arpeggios

1. F dominant ^{9} arpeggio

2. B$^\flat$ dominant ^{9} arpeggio

3. D dominant ^{9} arpeggio

4. E$^\flat$ dominant ^{9} arpeggio

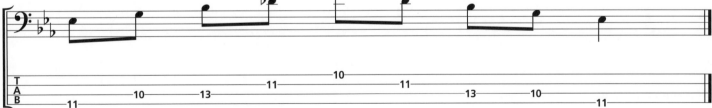

Grade 7 Technical Exercises

Group D: Chords | Dominant⁷ chords

1. E dominant⁷ chord

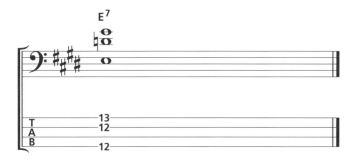

2. A dominant⁷ chord

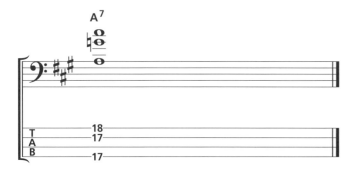

Group D: Chords | Minor⁷ chords

1. E minor⁷ chord

2. A minor⁷ chord

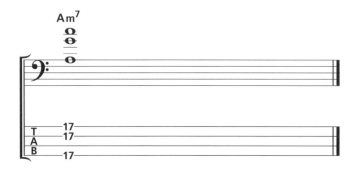

Group D: Chords | Major⁷ chords

1. E major⁷ chord

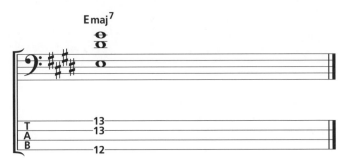

2. A major⁷ chord

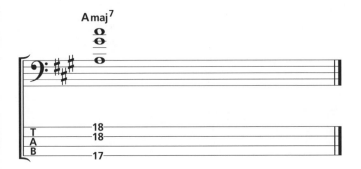

Grade 7 Technical Exercises

Group E: Stylistic Studies

You will prepare a technical study from one group of styles from the list below. Your choice of style will determine the style of the Quick Study Piece.

1. Rock/Metal: pedal tones and legato phrasing

CD Tracks 13 & 14

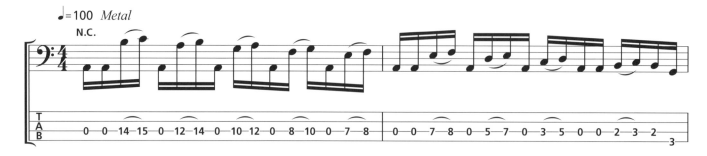

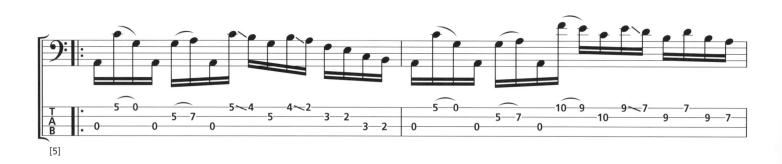

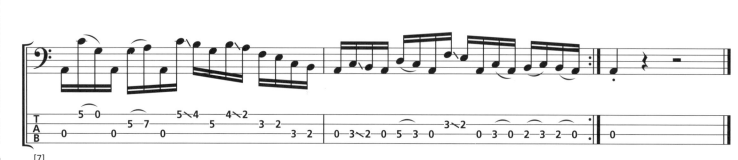

2. Funk: 16th-note slap grooves and string crossing

CD Tracks 15 & 16

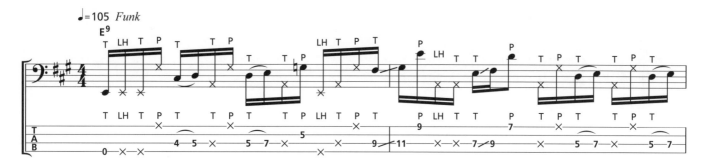

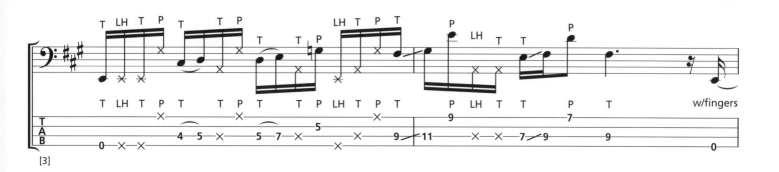

[3]

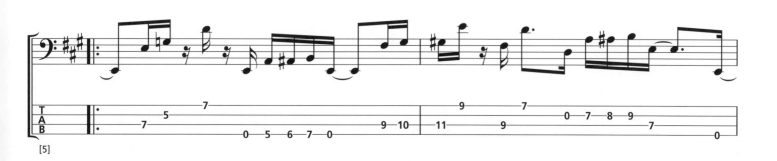

[5]

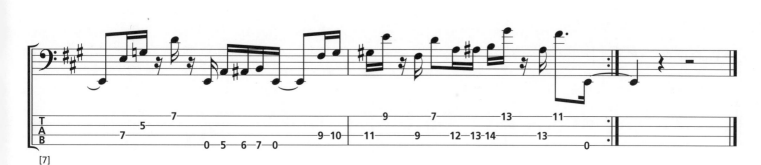

[7]

3. Jazz/Latin/Blues: natural harmonics and arpeggios

CD Tracks 17 & 18

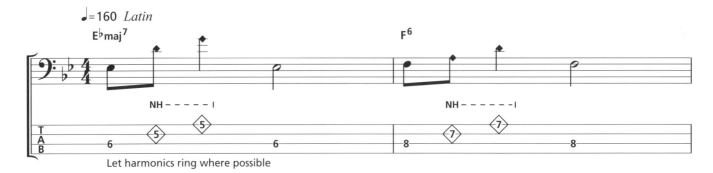

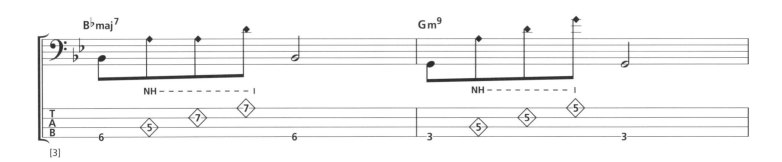

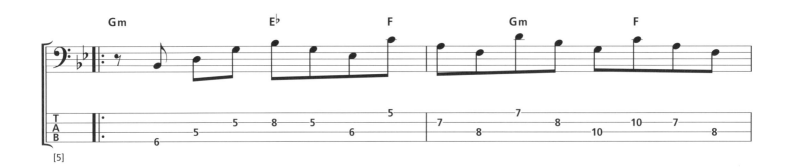

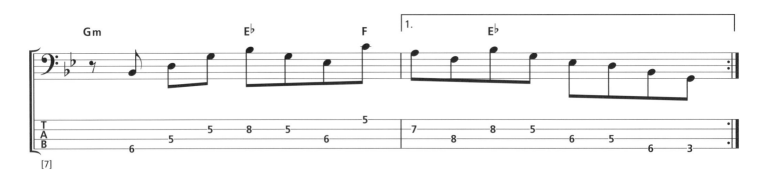

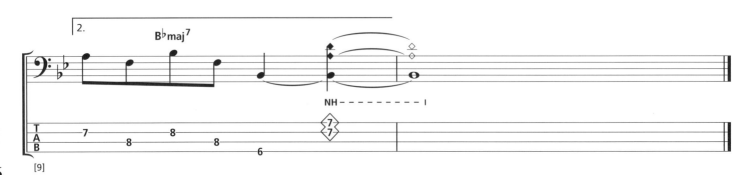

Grade 8

Grade 8 features three new scale types (whole tone, diminished and altered) in two fingerings from four starting notes. The natural minor is required over two octaves in one key. Four new arpeggio types (dominant $7\sharp5$, dominant $7\flat5$, dominant $7\sharp9$ and dominant $7\flat9$) are required from two starting notes. The three chord types found in Grade 7 remain the same, but use different fingerings. The Stylistic Studies follow the same procedure as previous grades.

Technical Work	
Tempo	♩= 100 (♫ played)
Scales | Whole Tone	F#/G♭, G, G#/A♭, & C#/D♭
Scales | Diminished	F#/G♭, G, G#/A♭, & C#/D♭
Scales | Altered	F#/G♭, G, G#/A♭, & C#/D♭
Scales | Natural Minor	G
Arpeggios | Dominant $7\sharp5$	D & G
Arpeggios | Dominant $7\flat5$	D & G
Arpeggios | Dominant $7\sharp9$	D & G
Arpeggios | Dominant $7\flat9$	D & G
Chords | Dominant 7	F#/G♭, G, G#/A♭, & C#/D♭
Chords | Minor 7	F#/G♭, G, G#/A♭, & C#/D♭
Chords | Major 7	F#/G♭, G, G#/A♭, & C#/D♭
Stylistic Studies	Rock/Metal Funk Jazz/Latin/Blues

Grade 8 Technical Exercises

Group A: Scales | Whole tone scales

1. F♯ whole tone scale

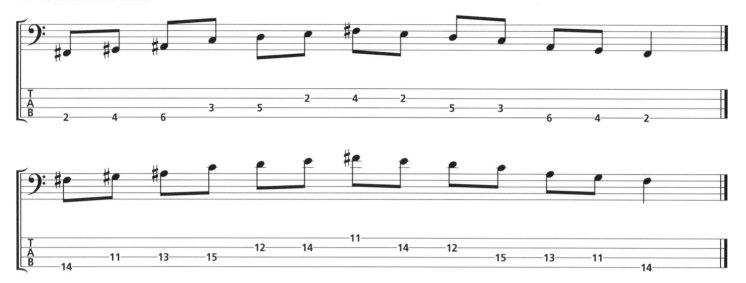

2. G whole tone scale

3. G♯ whole tone scale

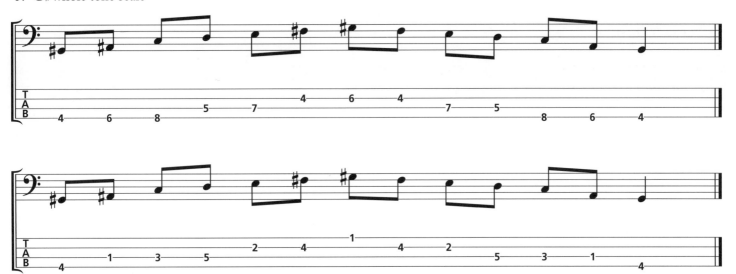

4. C♯ whole tone scale

Grade 8 Technical Exercises

Group A: Scales | Diminished scales

1. F♯ diminished scale

2. G diminished scale

3. G# diminished scale

4. C# diminished scale

Grade 8 Technical Exercises

Group A: Scales | Altered scales

1. F♯ altered scale

2. G altered scale

3. G♯ altered scale

4. C♯ altered scale

Group B: Scales | Natural minor scales

1. G natural minor scale

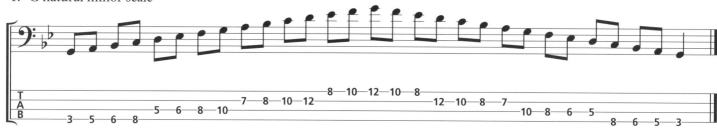

Group C: Arpeggios | Dominant $7\sharp5$ arpeggios

1. D dominant $7\sharp5$

2. G dominant $7\sharp5$

Group C: Arpeggios | Dominant $7\flat5$ arpeggios

1. D dominant $7\flat5$

2. G dominant $7\flat5$

Grade 8 Technical Exercises

Group C: Arpeggios | Dominant $7\sharp9$ arpeggios

1. D dominant $7\sharp9$

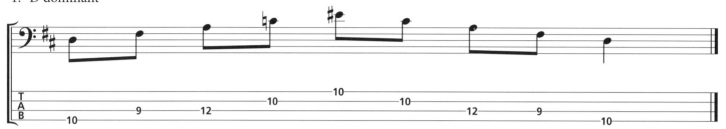

2. G dominant $7\sharp9$

Group C: Arpeggios | Dominant $7\flat9$ arpeggios

1. D dominant $7\flat9$

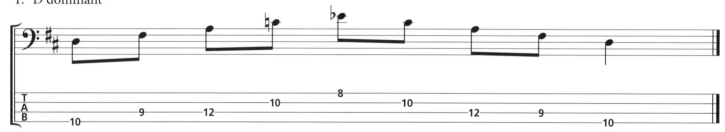

2. G dominant $7\flat9$

Group D: Chords | Dominant ⁷ chords

1. F♯ dominant ⁷

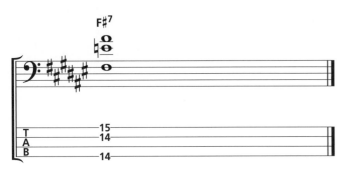

2. G dominant ⁷

3. D♭ dominant ⁷

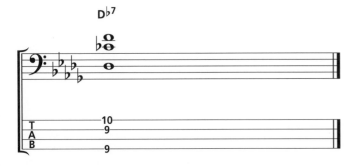

4. A♭ dominant ⁷

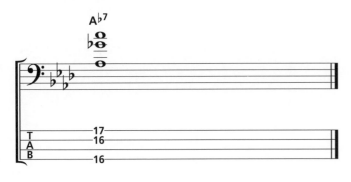

Grade 8 Technical Exercises

Group D: Chords | Minor 7 chords

1. F# minor 7

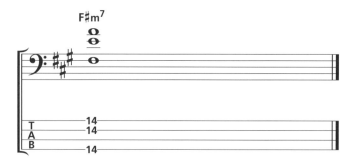

2. G minor 7

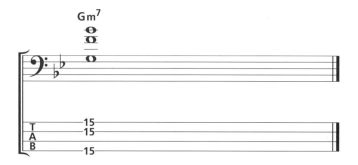

3. C# minor 7

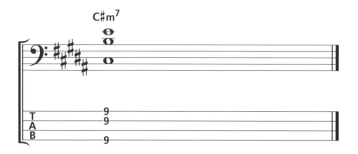

4. A♭ minor 7

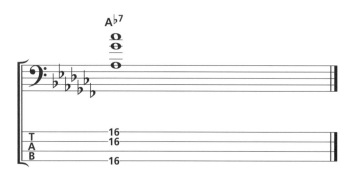

Bass Technical Handbook

108

Group D: Chords | Major⁷ chords

1. F♯ major⁷

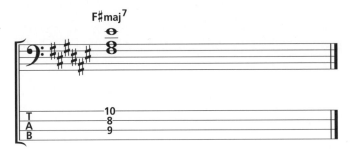

2. G major⁷

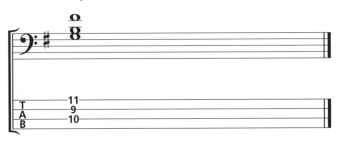

3. D♭ major⁷

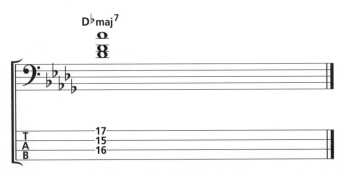

4. A♭ major⁷

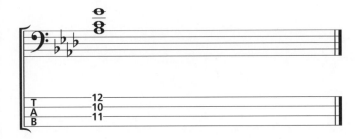

Grade 8 Technical Exercises

Group E: Stylistic Studies

You will prepare a technical study from one group of styles from the list below. Your choice of style will determine the style of the Quick Study Piece.

1. Rock/Metal: odd-time grooves and powerchords

CD Tracks 19 & 20

[3]

[5]

[8]

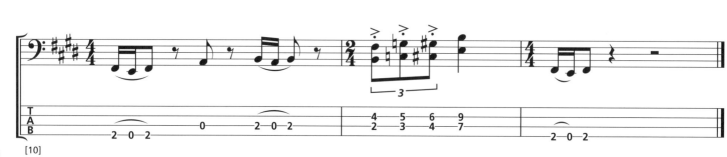

[10]

2. Funk: syncopation and slap bass technique

3. Jazz/Latin/Blues: uptempo fingerstyle technique and walking basslines